CHAPTER 1: INTRODUCTION

Welcome to the transformative journey toward financial freedom! If you've picked up this book, congratulations on taking the first step toward becoming a Chill Millionaire. This guide is designed to help you liberate yourself from the shackles of debt, providing practical tips and actionable strategies to pave the way for a life of abundance and relaxation.

We understand that the road to financial freedom might seem daunting, but with the right mindset and a solid plan, you can achieve your goals. Whether you're drowning in debt, looking to enhance your financial well-being, or aspiring to become a Chill Millionaire, this guide is tailored to meet you where you are.

The Chill Millionaire Mindset

At the core of this journey lies the Chill Millionaire mindset — a unique approach to wealth that prioritizes both financial stability and a relaxed, fulfilling lifestyle. This mindset isn't just about accumulating wealth for the sake of it but understanding the importance of balance, peace of mind, and enjoying the journey.

In this section, we'll delve into the key principles of the Chill Millionaire mindset:

1. Holistic Wealth
Acknowledging that wealth extends beyond monetary value to include physical, mental, and emotional well-being.

2. Intentional Living
Making conscious choices about how you spend, save, and invest your resources to align with your values and long-term goals.

3. Financial Mindfulness
Cultivating awareness of your financial habits, understanding the impact of your decisions, and making informed choices.

4. Gratitude and Abundance
Focusing on what you have, expressing gratitude, and recognizing the abundance in your life, fostering a positive relationship with money.

5. Life Enjoyment
Embracing the present moment, finding joy in simple pleasures, and avoiding the trap of constant, unfulfilling consumption.

As you embark on this journey, keep these principles in mind. The Chill Millionaire mindset will serve as your compass, guiding you through the practical strategies and steps outlined in the chapters ahead. It's not just about reaching financial milestones; it's about crafting a life that aligns with your values, passions, and the peace of mind that comes with being debt-free and financially secure. So, let's dive in and start building the foundation for your Chill Millionaire lifestyle!

CHAPTER 2: ASSESSING YOUR CURRENT FINANCIAL SITUATION

A. UNDERSTANDING YOUR DEBT

1. Types of Debt

Why it Matters:
Before embarking on the path to financial freedom, you must acquaint yourself with the types of debt you're carrying. Each type comes with its own set of challenges and considerations.

Practical Steps:
- **List Your Debts:** Create a comprehensive list of all your debts, including credit cards, student loans, mortgages, and personal loans.
- **Categorize Your Debts:** Differentiate between high-interest and low-interest debts to prioritize repayment.

Insightful Tips:

- **Know Your Interest Rates:** Understand the interest rates associated with each debt to strategize your repayment plan effectively.
- **Acknowledge the Purpose:** Reflect on the reasons behind each debt, helping you make informed decisions about your financial priorities.

2. Calculating Total Debt

Why it Matters:
To develop a successful debt repayment plan, you need a clear understanding of your overall debt load. This step is crucial for setting realistic goals and timelines.

Practical Steps:
- **Gather Statements:** Collect all statements for your debts, ensuring you have accurate and up-to-date information.
- **Include Accrued Interest:** Calculate the total debt by considering both principal amounts and any accrued interest.

Insightful Tips:
- **Regular Updates:** Periodically revisit and recalculate your total debt to stay informed about your progress.
- **Celebrate Milestones:** Acknowledge and celebrate achievements as you gradually reduce your total debt.

B. EVALUATING YOUR INCOME AND EXPENSES

1. Creating a Budget

Why it Matters:
Budgeting is the foundation of financial stability, providing a roadmap for managing your money wisely.

Practical Steps:
- **List Your Income Sources:** Identify all sources of income, ensuring you include regular and irregular streams.
- **Categorize Expenses:** Classify your expenses into fixed and variable categories for better control.

Insightful Tips:
- **Emergency Fund Allocation:** Allocate a portion of your budget to building and maintaining an emergency fund.
- **Be Realistic:** Set achievable budget goals to avoid frustration and maintain long-term commitment.

2. Identifying Areas for Improvement

Why it Matters:
Optimizing income and minimizing unnecessary expenses is key to effective financial management.

Practical Steps:
- **Expense Audit:** Review your expenses to identify areas where you can cut back or reallocate funds.
- **Negotiation Strategies:** Explore negotiation opportunities for bills, subscriptions, and regular expenses.

Insightful Tips:
- **Incremental Adjustments:** Make gradual changes to your

spending habits to ensure sustainability.
- **Explore Additional Income:** Investigate side hustles or creative ways to increase your income.

By the end of this chapter, you'll have a comprehensive understanding of your financial landscape. Armed with this knowledge, you'll be well-equipped to move on to the next steps in your journey toward becoming a Chill Millionaire: creating a debt repayment plan and setting the stage for sustainable financial success. Remember, the key is to approach this process with curiosity and a commitment to positive change. Let's get started on your path to financial freedom!

CHAPTER 3: CREATING A DEBT REPAYMENT PLAN

A. PRIORITIZING DEBTS

1. High-Interest vs. Low-Interest Debt

Why it Matters:
Understanding the impact of interest rates is pivotal for an effective debt repayment strategy. High-interest debts can accumulate quickly, hindering your path to financial freedom.

Practical Steps
- **List Your Debts by Interest Rate:** Arrange your debts in descending order based on interest rates.
- **Allocate Repayment Focus:** Prioritize paying off high-interest debts first to minimize overall interest payments.

Insightful Tips:
- **Snowball Effect:** Consider the psychological boost of paying off smaller debts first, even if they have lower interest rates.
- **Long-Term Savings:** Focusing on high-interest debts initially

can lead to significant long-term savings.

2. Snowball vs. Avalanche Method

Why it Matters:
Choosing the right repayment method aligns with your financial personality and motivates you throughout the debt repayment journey.

Practical Steps:
- **Snowball Method:** Pay off debts from smallest to largest regardless of interest rates.
- **Avalanche Method:** Tackle debts with the highest interest rates first, regardless of the balance.

Insightful Tips:
- **Emotional Motivation:** The Snowball Method can provide a sense of accomplishment, while the Avalanche Method saves more money in the long run.
- **Hybrid Approach:** Customize your strategy by combining elements of both methods for a balanced approach.

B. NEGOTIATING INTEREST RATES AND REPAYMENT TERMS

Why it Matters:
Negotiating can significantly ease the burden of debt repayment, making it more manageable and affordable.

Practical Steps:
- **Research Current Interest Rates:** Understand the prevailing interest rates for your types of debts.
- **Contact Your Creditors:** Initiate conversations with creditors to negotiate lower interest rates or favorable repayment terms.

Insightful Tips:
- **Be Prepared:** Arm yourself with knowledge about your financial situation before negotiating.
- **Professional Guidance:** If negotiations seem challenging, consider seeking advice from financial counselors or debt consolidation services.

C. SETTING REALISTIC REPAYMENT GOALS

Why it Matters:
Setting achievable goals helps maintain motivation and ensures steady progress toward debt freedom.

Practical Steps:
- **Assess Your Budget:** Determine how much you can realistically allocate toward debt repayment each month.
- **Establish Milestones:** Break down your total debt into manageable milestones with target dates.

Insightful Tips:
- **Flexibility is Key:** Life is unpredictable; build flexibility into your goals to accommodate unexpected expenses.
- **Celebrate Achievements:** Acknowledge and celebrate each milestone, reinforcing your commitment to the debt repayment journey.

By implementing these practical steps and insightful tips, you'll be well on your way to creating a personalized debt repayment plan. Remember, the key is to choose a strategy that aligns with your financial situation and motivates you for the long haul. Let's move forward, take control of your financial destiny, and pave the way to a debt-free and chill millionaire lifestyle!

CHAPTER 4: BUILDING A CHILL MILLIONAIRE EMERGENCY FUND

A. IMPORTANCE OF AN EMERGENCY FUND

Why it Matters:
An emergency fund is your financial safety net, providing peace of mind and protection against unexpected expenses. Understanding its significance is crucial for a stable financial foundation.

Practical Steps:
- **Identify Potential Emergencies:** Consider scenarios such as medical expenses, car repairs, or job loss.
- **Learn from Past Experiences:** Reflect on previous emergencies to gauge the importance of having a financial buffer.

Insightful Tips:
- **Stress Reduction:** An emergency fund reduces financial stress,

allowing you to navigate unexpected situations with greater ease.
- **Preserving Financial Goals:** It prevents you from derailing long-term financial goals when faced with sudden expenses.

B. DETERMINING THE RIGHT SIZE FOR YOUR FUND

Why it Matters:

Knowing the appropriate size for your emergency fund ensures you have sufficient coverage without tying up excess funds unnecessarily.

Practical Steps:

- **Evaluate Monthly Expenses:** Calculate your essential monthly expenses, including bills, groceries, and debt repayments.
- **Multiply by Months:** Aim for 3 to 6 months' worth of expenses as a general guideline for your emergency fund size.

Insightful Tips:

- **Personalize Your Fund:** Consider factors such as job stability, health, and lifestyle to determine whether a larger or smaller fund is appropriate.
- **Regular Review:** Periodically reassess your fund size as circumstances, expenses, and income may change over time.

C. WHERE TO PARK YOUR EMERGENCY FUND

Why it Matters:

Choosing the right location for your emergency fund involves balancing accessibility and potential returns.

Practical Steps:

- **Explore Savings Accounts:** Opt for high-yield savings accounts with easy access and minimal fees.
- **Consider Money Market Accounts:** These accounts offer slightly higher interest rates while maintaining liquidity.

Insightful Tips:

- **Separate from Daily Accounts**: Keep your emergency fund separate from your regular checking account to avoid accidental spending.
- **Accessibility Matters**: Prioritize accounts that allow quick access to funds when needed.

By understanding the importance of an emergency fund, determining the right size, and strategically placing your funds, you're building a solid financial foundation. The goal is not just to weather unexpected storms but to do so while maintaining your Chill Millionaire mindset. As you embark on this chapter, remember that financial stability is a journey, and the steps you take now contribute to a more relaxed and secure future. Let's continue building toward your financial goals!

CHAPTER 5: INVESTING FOR LONG-TERM WEALTH

A. INTRODUCTION TO INVESTING

Why it Matters:

Investing is a powerful tool for building wealth over the long term. This section introduces you to the fundamentals of investing, emphasizing its role in achieving financial freedom.

Practical Steps:

- **Understand the Purpose of Investing:** Clarify your financial goals and how investing aligns with achieving them.
- **Risk Tolerance Assessment:** Evaluate your risk tolerance to tailor your investment strategy to your comfort level.

Insightful Tips:

- **Start Early:** The earlier you begin investing, the more time your money has to grow through compounding.
- **Educate Yourself:** Stay informed about investment vehicles, market trends, and economic factors influencing your investments.

B. TYPES OF INVESTMENTS

1. Stocks

Why it Matters:
Stocks represent ownership in a company and have the potential for significant returns, albeit with higher volatility.

Practical Steps:
- **Research Companies:** Understand the basics of companies you're interested in, including their financial health and market position.
- **Diversify Stock Holdings:** Spread investments across various industries to minimize risk.

Insightful Tips:
- **Long-Term Perspective:** Stocks are well-suited for long-term investors; avoid reacting to short-term market fluctuations.
- **Dividend Stocks:** Consider dividend-paying stocks for a source of regular income.

2. Bonds

Why it Matters:
Bonds are debt securities that provide a more stable but lower-return investment compared to stocks.

Practical Steps:
- **Learn About Bond Types:** Understand government bonds, corporate bonds, and municipal bonds.
- **Assess Risk Levels:** Bonds vary in risk; choose based on your risk

tolerance and investment goals.

Insightful Tips:
- **Diversification:** Including bonds in your portfolio adds stability during market volatility.
- **Interest Rate Considerations:** Be aware of interest rate movements, as they can impact bond values.

3. Real Estate

Why it Matters:
Real estate offers a tangible and potentially lucrative investment opportunity, diversifying your portfolio.

Practical Steps:
- **Research Property Markets:** Understand the dynamics of the real estate market in areas of interest.
- **Consider Rental Income:** If applicable, evaluate the potential for rental income.

Insightful Tips:
- **Location is Key:** The value of real estate often depends on its location.
- **Risk Mitigation:** Real estate can act as a hedge against inflation and stock market fluctuations.

C. BUILDING A DIVERSE INVESTMENT PORTFOLIO

Why it Matters:
Diversification is the key to reducing risk and optimizing returns in your investment portfolio.

Practical Steps:
- **Allocate Across Asset Classes:** Balance your portfolio by distributing investments across stocks, bonds, and real estate.
- **Regularly Rebalance:** Adjust your portfolio periodically to maintain your desired asset allocation.

Insightful Tips:
- **Stay Informed:** Keep abreast of market trends and economic indicators influencing different asset classes.
- **Seek Professional Advice:** Consider consulting with a financial advisor to tailor your investment strategy to your specific circumstances.

As you embark on your investment journey, remember that building wealth through investments is a gradual process. By gaining a solid understanding of investment basics, exploring different types of investments, and maintaining a diversified portfolio, you're laying the groundwork for long-term financial success. Keep your Chill Millionaire mindset intact and let your investments work for you over time. Let's dive into the exciting world of long-term wealth building!

CHAPTER 6: SIDE HUSTLES AND PASSIVE INCOME STREAMS

A. IDENTIFYING YOUR SKILLS AND PASSIONS

Why it Matters:
Unlocking the potential of side hustles and passive income begins with recognizing your unique skills and passions. This section guides you in pinpointing what you excel at and what brings you fulfillment.

Practical Steps:
- **Skill Inventory:** List your skills, both professional and personal.
- **Passion Reflection:** Identify activities that genuinely excite and motivate you.

Insightful Tips:

- **Combine Skills and Passions:** Look for intersections where your skills align with your passions.
- **Leverage Hobbies:** Hobbies can often be turned into profitable side hustles.

B. EXPLORING DIFFERENT SIDE HUSTLE OPPORTUNITIES

Why it Matters:
Diversifying your income through side hustles provides financial flexibility and potential growth. This section offers practical suggestions for discovering viable side hustle opportunities.

Practical Steps:
- **Market Research:** Identify demands in the market for specific services or products.
- **Assess Time Commitment:** Choose side hustles that align with your schedule and energy levels.

Insightful Tips:
- **Gig Economy Opportunities:** Explore freelancing, consulting, or participating in gig platforms.
- **Online Platforms:** Leverage websites and apps that connect freelancers with clients for diverse side hustle opportunities.

C. INVESTING IN PASSIVE INCOME STREAMS

Why it Matters:

Passive income streams generate revenue with minimal ongoing effort, providing financial stability and freedom. This section outlines various avenues for building passive income.

Practical Steps:

- **Real Estate Investments:** Consider rental properties or real estate crowdfunding platforms.
- **Dividend Stocks:** Invest in stocks that pay regular dividends.
- **Create Digital Products:** Develop and sell e-books, courses, or digital art.

Insightful Tips:

- **Diversification:** Spread your passive income sources to minimize risk.
- **Continuous Improvement:** Regularly evaluate and enhance your passive income strategies.

By identifying your skills and passions, exploring side hustle opportunities, and investing in passive income streams, you're setting the stage for a more resilient and financially abundant future. This chapter encourages you to not only diversify your income sources but also find fulfillment in the process. Keep the Chill Millionaire mindset alive as you explore these opportunities, and remember, every additional income stream is a step closer to your financial goals. Let's embrace the world of side hustles and passive income together!

CHAPTER 7: LIFESTYLE ADJUSTMENTS FOR FINANCIAL FREEDOM

A. DIFFERENTIATING BETWEEN NEEDS AND WANTS

Why it Matters:
Distinguishing between needs and wants is fundamental to achieving financial freedom. This section helps you develop a keen awareness of your spending habits.

Practical Steps:
- **Create a Necessities List:** Identify essential expenses required for a comfortable life.
- **Evaluate Non-Essential Spending:** Scrutinize your discretionary expenses and classify them as wants.

Insightful Tips:

- **Mindful Decision-Making:** Before making a purchase, pause and ask yourself if it's a need or a want.
- **Cultivate Contentment:** Focus on appreciating what you have, reducing the desire for unnecessary purchases.

B. SMART SPENDING HABITS

Why it Matters:
Developing smart spending habits ensures that your money works for you rather than against you. This section provides actionable tips for optimizing your spending.

Practical Steps:
- **Budgeting for Fun:** Allocate a specific amount for discretionary spending to avoid impulsive decisions.
- **Comparison Shopping:** Explore different options and compare prices before making significant purchases.

Insightful Tips:
- **Delayed Gratification:** Implement a waiting period for non-essential purchases to reduce impulse buying.
- **Set Spending Limits:** Establish limits for various spending categories to maintain financial discipline.

C. LIVING BELOW YOUR MEANS

Why it Matters:
Living below your means is a cornerstone of financial freedom, enabling you to save and invest for the future. This section guides

you on adopting a sustainable lifestyle within your financial capacity.

Practical Steps:

- **Savings as a Priority:** Allocate a portion of your income to savings before considering discretionary spending.
- **Regular Expense Audits:** Periodically review your expenses to identify areas where you can cut back.

Insightful Tips:

- **Mindful Upgrades:** Before upgrading, assess if the improvement significantly enhances your quality of life.
- **Track Your Progress:** Monitor your journey to living below your means and celebrate milestones along the way.

By understanding the distinction between needs and wants, cultivating smart spending habits, and adopting a lifestyle that allows you to live below your means, you are actively shaping a financial future of freedom and abundance. This chapter encourages a mindful approach to spending, enabling you to redirect your resources toward meaningful financial goals. Embrace the journey of conscious living and financial empowerment, embodying the essence of the Chill Millionaire mindset. Let's make intentional lifestyle adjustments for a more fulfilling and financially liberated life!

CHAPTER 8: OVERCOMING FINANCIAL CHALLENGES

A. DEALING WITH UNEXPECTED EXPENSES

Why it Matters:
Life is unpredictable, and unexpected expenses can derail even the most well-laid financial plans. This section equips you with strategies to handle unforeseen financial challenges effectively.

Practical Steps:
- **Emergency Fund Utilization:** Tap into your emergency fund for genuine emergencies.
- **Prioritize Expenses:** Identify non-essential expenses that can be temporarily reduced to accommodate unexpected costs.

Insightful Tips:

- **Negotiation Skills:** When facing unexpected bills, negotiate payment plans or seek discounts where possible.
- **Learn from the Experience:** Use unexpected expenses as opportunities to refine your budget and emergency planning.

B. COPING WITH INCOME FLUCTUATIONS

Why it Matters:
Income fluctuations are common, and navigating through them is essential for maintaining financial stability. This section provides strategies to cope with varying income levels.

Practical Steps:
- **Create a Variable Budget:** Design a budget that can adapt to fluctuations in income.
- **Build a Financial Buffer:** Save during high-income periods to cushion the impact of low-income periods.

Insightful Tips:
- **Diversify Income Sources:** Explore additional streams of income to mitigate the impact of a reduction in one source.
- **Regular Financial Check-ins:** Conduct regular reviews of your budget to adjust for changes in income.

C. STAYING MOTIVATED DURING THE JOURNEY

Why it Matters:

Maintaining motivation is crucial for staying on course towards financial freedom. This section provides strategies to keep your enthusiasm alive throughout the journey.

Practical Steps:
- **Set Achievable Goals:** Break down long-term goals into smaller, achievable milestones.
- **Visualize Success:** Create a vision board or regularly reflect on the positive outcomes of your financial journey.

Insightful Tips:
- **Celebrate Small Wins:** Acknowledge and celebrate every achievement, no matter how small.
- **Community Support:** Share your financial goals with a supportive community to stay motivated and accountable.

By preparing for unexpected expenses, adapting to income fluctuations, and staying motivated throughout your financial journey, you'll be better equipped to overcome challenges and stay on the path to financial freedom. Remember, setbacks are a natural part of the process, and how you respond to them shapes your financial resilience. Cultivate a positive mindset, learn from experiences, and use challenges as stepping stones toward your Chill Millionaire lifestyle. Let's face financial challenges with confidence and determination!

CHAPTER 9: CELEBRATING FINANCIAL MILESTONES

A. SETTING AND ACHIEVING SHORT-TERM GOALS

Why it Matters:
Setting short-term financial goals provides a roadmap to your larger objectives. This section guides you in establishing realistic milestones and achieving them incrementally.

Practical Steps:
- **Define Specific Goals:** Clearly articulate short-term financial objectives with measurable outcomes.
- **Break Down Larger Goals:** Divide bigger goals into smaller, manageable tasks to enhance achievability.

Insightful Tips:
- **Prioritize Goals:** Rank your goals based on urgency and significance.
- **Flexible Adjustments:** Be willing to adjust goals as

circumstances change while maintaining a forward trajectory.

B. RECOGNIZING ACHIEVEMENTS ALONG THE WAY

Why it Matters:
Acknowledging your progress boosts motivation and reinforces positive financial habits. This section provides strategies to recognize and celebrate achievements.

Practical Steps:
- **Create a Milestone Tracker:** Develop a visual representation of your progress toward each goal.
- **Reward System:** Establish a reward system for reaching milestones, aligning with your values and budget.

Insightful Tips:
- **Reflect on Growth:** Take time to reflect on the skills and knowledge gained during your financial journey.
- **Share Achievements:** Celebrate milestones with friends or family to enhance the sense of accomplishment.

C. BUILDING A POSITIVE RELATIONSHIP WITH MONEY

Why it Matters:
Cultivating a positive relationship with money fosters a healthier

financial mindset. This section encourages you to view money as a tool for empowerment rather than a source of stress.

Practical Steps:
- **Regular Financial Check-ins:** Review your financial goals and progress periodically to stay connected with your financial journey.
- **Educate Yourself:** Increase financial literacy to make informed decisions and reduce anxiety about money matters.

Insightful Tips:
- **Gratitude Practice:** Express gratitude for your financial accomplishments, no matter how small.
- **Mindful Spending:** Align your spending with your values, reinforcing a positive connection with money.

By setting and achieving short-term goals, recognizing achievements, and fostering a positive relationship with money, you're creating a sustainable and fulfilling financial journey. Celebrate the milestones along the way, as they signify progress towards your ultimate Chill Millionaire lifestyle. Remember, the key is not just reaching financial goals but also embracing the positive transformations occurring within yourself. Let's continue the journey of financial celebration and empowerment!

CHAPTER 10: SUSTAINING YOUR CHILL MILLIONAIRE LIFESTYLE

A. MAINTAINING FINANCIAL DISCIPLINE

Why it Matters:
Maintaining financial discipline is crucial for sustaining the Chill Millionaire lifestyle. This section provides strategies to stay disciplined and avoid common pitfalls.

Practical Steps:
- **Stick to Your Budget:** Regularly review and adhere to your budget to ensure financial stability.
- **Emergency Fund Maintenance:** Continue contributing to and maintaining your emergency fund for unexpected expenses.

Insightful Tips:
- **Mindful Spending Habits:** Be intentional about your spending, focusing on needs over wants.
- **Automate Savings:** Set up automatic transfers to savings and investment accounts to enforce consistent financial discipline.

B. REGULARLY REVIEWING AND ADJUSTING YOUR FINANCIAL PLAN

Why it Matters:
Financial plans should evolve with changing circumstances. This section guides you in regularly reviewing and adjusting your plan to align with your current goals.

Practical Steps:
- **Quarterly Reviews:** Conduct comprehensive reviews of your financial plan at least quarterly.
- **Adjust Goals as Needed:** Modify your short-term and long-term goals based on changes in income, expenses, and life circumstances.

Insightful Tips:
- **Celebrate Progress:** Use regular reviews as an opportunity to celebrate achievements and reassess priorities.
- **Emergency Fund Adjustments:** Adjust the size of your emergency fund based on changes in your financial situation.

C. INSPIRING OTHERS TO ACHIEVE

FINANCIAL FREEDOM

Why it Matters:
Sharing your journey and inspiring others to achieve financial freedom not only benefits them but reinforces your commitment to the Chill Millionaire lifestyle.

Practical Steps:
- **Share Your Story:** Communicate your financial journey, including challenges and successes, with friends and family.
- **Offer Guidance:** Provide support and guidance to those interested in improving their financial well-being.

Insightful Tips:
- **Lead by Example:** Demonstrate the positive changes in your life resulting from financial freedom.
- **Encourage Small Steps:** Inspire others to take small, achievable steps toward their financial goals.

By maintaining financial discipline, regularly reviewing and adjusting your financial plan, and inspiring others to achieve financial freedom, you're not just living the Chill Millionaire lifestyle; you're actively contributing to a culture of financial empowerment. This chapter emphasizes the long-term nature of financial freedom and the importance of continuous improvement. As you sustain your Chill Millionaire lifestyle, remember that the journey is ongoing, and each step you take contributes to a more relaxed and fulfilling financial future. Let's continue this journey with commitment, wisdom, and a positive impact on others!

CHAPTER 11: CONCLUSION

As you conclude this guide, remember that the path to financial freedom is a continuous journey. Challenges will arise, circumstances will change, and your financial goals may evolve. Stay committed to the principles outlined here, be adaptable in your approach, and celebrate both the small victories and significant milestones.

Becoming a Chill Millionaire is not just about achieving financial goals; it's a holistic approach to life. It's about finding balance, embracing abundance, and enjoying the journey. Your path to financial freedom is unique, and by integrating the strategies and principles outlined in this guide, you're well on your way to a Chill Millionaire lifestyle.

May your financial journey be filled with wisdom, resilience, and a sense of fulfillment. As you embark on this adventure, remember that true wealth extends beyond dollars and cents. It encompasses well-being, joy, and the freedom to live life on your terms. Here's to your Chill Millionaire lifestyle — a life of abundance, peace, and financial freedom!